From
GOD
To
ME

Sonia Beckwith

ISBN 978-1-64079-194-7 (Paperback)
ISBN 978-1-64079-195-4 (Digital)

Christian Faith Publishing, Inc.
296 Chestnut Street
Meadville, PA 16335
www.christianfaithpublishing.com

Printed in the United States of America

LIE PASSIVE IN GOD'S HANDS, AND
TO KNOW NO WILL BUT HIS

William S. Plumer, 1802-1880

Introduction

To fully understand the Word of God, we must read it knowing the Old Testament points to the cross and the New Testament points to the life of Jesus and back to the cross. We also must ask key questions such as, what was the culture of the day, or what was the problem being addressed? When reading *From God to Me*, I am sure you will find that some of the scriptures I used are taken out of context. But I know/believe that God (being God) does use his word out of context for us. I know this because he has for me. However, I am wise enough to know I cannot take this out-of-context message God spoke to my heart and make some new truth for you to claim. God's Word is complete, and we cannot add to or take away from it.

I have said so many times and will continue saying: ANY good that comes from me is only because God placed it in me. I am not capable on my own! I have seen myself a willing sinner. Not just born of a sin nature, but one who selfishly acts to her benefit to satisfy her own self. **I have struggled my entire life with myself.** But I know God will complete in me what he started unto the day of redemption. The race set before me will be accomplished.

The one motto I have lived by: "You are never a failure unless when you fall, you don't stand back up."

The first time I heard these words, I saw myself walking down the path of life falling, tripping, getting scraped up, bruised, and bloody. I saw myself dirty and dusty with one knee on the ground, holding my elbow while in motion trying to stand one more time. I could see myself taking a long deep breath, saying,

"Come on, Sonia, let's try this again. Get up and keep walking, for the Kingdom of God is worth it." And with every fall, I saw Jesus right there beside me, bent down, leaning in, with his arm wrapped around my waist, helping me up. The Victor of Life helping His wounded soldier!

Dedication

Foremost without hesitation, I give honor to God, who sent his Son to show us the way back to His heart; His love for man, forever tearing the curtain and opening up the most Holy of holies so each and every one of us, upon accepting Jesus as the atonement for our sin, can experience His love! It is absolutely the sweetest place you will ever want to be.

However, the desire to write has been for my children and my family. I have this great longing for them to know the thread of my life: Christ! God deserves so much more than what my life has shown. It is so easy to remember the mess-ups and failures of life. The negatives seem to ring louder than the positives. I guess because hurt runs deep. Along with my children and family, I pray that if you do not know the reason God sent Jesus, the Holy Spirit will grab hold of your soul and open your spiritual eyes to your need of the cross.

I pray, Benjamin, Sarah, and Daniel, as you read my heart, you will look past my faults and my sinful nature and see Christ! I wish when each of you were born I already had the wisdom of a ninety-year-old woman. I would have been such a better mother. It is so much clearer looking backward than forward. I am blessed to have all three of you in my life:

Benjamin: my first born!
Sarah: my daughter!
Daniel: my baby! (Sorry, son, it is your birth order.)
I love you!

Special Thanks To:

Judith Hebb, PhD: Without your professional suggestions and initial edit of my book, I doubt I would have had the confidence to send my manuscript to Christian Faith Publishing. You are a remarkable woman with many amazing gifts. Many thanks!!

Thank you to my good friend and brother in Christ Tony who came along side me and pushed my book over the finish line. You are rich in the things of our Lord! You are a remarkable man and dedicated servant of our Lord and Savior Jesus! Many thanks!

The Rubber Pants

The commandments "do not commit adultery," "Do not murder," "Do not steal," "Do not covet"...

—Romans 13:9

My first memory of the Holy Spirit was around age four. However, it is only now as I think back on my life that I know it was the Holy Spirit. My dad had an army buddy he stayed in touch with, and during one of those visits, I was playing with their daughter's doll. This doll was wearing "real" full-blown rubber pants; you know the kind you put over cloth diapers? And they were not the pretend ones that come with the doll. Somehow this girl's doll had on REAL ones, and I WANTED THEM. I can still remember to this day the **covetousness** of my heart. I desired those rubber pants, and I began thinking of a way to get them home with me. At age four, I knew I was doing something wrong and I had to hide it. So I went and put on my royal blue knee-length fur coat, and I took those rubber pants off her doll and slipped them in my coat pocket. I got them! I was happy! On my way to fulfillment! Home soon and on my doll forever!

It was not until I put those rubber pants on my doll that the Holy Spirit showed up! And boy, did He show up! There was NOT ONE second of enjoyment! I did not get to smile with a happy exhale of accomplishment. At age four I stood there looking at my doll with those perfect rubber pants on in total disbelief. My emotional jaw dropped to my knees and my arms were hanging in disgust of myself.

I just knew I would be happy seeing my doll in those rubber pants, but NOPE, not at all! I remember the emptiness, the numbness, the conviction of taking something from someone else, something that was not mine. There was absolutely no enjoyment! I quickly took those rubber pants off my doll, slipped them back into my coat pocket, and the very next time we went to see my dad's army buddy and family, I put those rubber pants back on that doll. That was it! The Holy Spirit sealed me that day. **Stealing** was wrong, and it grieved Him!

The experience with the Holy Spirit's discipline at age four was so profound it has ruled my actions ever since. When the Holy Spirit speaks to the heart of man, it changes from that moment forward.

And whatever other commandments there may be, are summed up in this one rule: "Love your neighbor as yourself." Love does no harm to its neighbor. Therefore love is the fulfillment of the law.
—Romans 13:10

Prayers

As a child and into young adulthood, I always bargained with God or offered up trade if I did not hold my position. This was to let God know I was serious. Bless my dog, she never knew, but when I was a young girl, she was one of my greatest loves and was often used in manipulative prayer: "God, if you will do this for me, then I will surely do this for you, and if I don't, then you can take my dog." As innocent as these prayers were, it did begin to breed an expectation as if God owed me something.

As an adult, we may not pray specifically like a young child, but down deep in the heart we do sort of. I mean, why not? God could. He can. He should. He has ALL the resources, so we breed an expectation for Him to do it the way that obviously seems to be the best way, right?

Well, when you go through a season in life when God is quiet and struggles seem overwhelming, you sort of have to grow up spiritually. When prayers seemingly continue to go "unanswered" no matter how hard you pray, how often you pray, or how many tears you have shed, you are faced with having to develop another understanding regarding prayer.

After exhausting every different possible scenario in my attempt to get God's attention through prayer, I finally came to the throne room of God on bended knee, broken with nothing to offer, depleted of self. I surrender! But then, goodness, I had to surrender my surrender because in surrendering, I felt "entitled" by my surrendering. I was brought to a place of complete inexistence of self. I finally just cried out, "I come with empty hands. I have nothing to offer or trade." As I was crying out these words, it dawned on me to say, "All I have is your Son." And then God spoke, "My Son is all I have ever wanted you to have … before you … before Me!"

I pray a lot! I will continue to pray. In fact, I love praying and talking with God and Jesus. I come often before God with many prayers. Sometimes I have the whole world lifted up to him. I pray for people I don't know who suffer with hunger, neglect, who are physically or mentally ill. I pray for our enemies and those in the enemy's camp who are innocent of his agenda. I will always continue to knock, seek, ask, and plead for people's salvation. I will continue to praise, worship, and dance before His throne, celebrating the life He has given me through His Son; and sometimes my prayers are quiet as I walk silently with Him. But I no longer barter with God. I no longer try and manipulate God. To tell the truth, it never worked anyways, not even once! Yet, another prayer, thankful that He knows best and holds His position.

Like newborn babies, crave pure spiritual milk, so that by it you may grow up in your salvation.

—1 Peter 2:2

The Fast

While they were worshiping the Lord and fasting ...
—Acts 35:2

With prayer and fasting ...
—Act 14:23

I was sent to a small Bible school about three hours from home at age seventeen. I was messed up with a much older guy, and my mom was wise enough to follow God's leading. I don't know all her struggles in sending me, but I know she obeyed the Lord in the face of opposition.

This guy was about nine years older than me and had a serious hold on me. I look back on it now and believe it bordered on demonic oppression. He could have had a harem of girls, and yet somehow he made me believe I was his only one.

When my daughter reached the same age I was when I was having a relationship with him, I became very angry. I saw myself through my daughter being preyed upon. I could see in her my naïveté and the harm of a much older man. I saw ME and the manipulation of HIM. I don't think I ever despised anyone before this point.

When I first arrived at this school, of course, all I thought about was him and getting back to him. But it did not take very long before he soon faded to the normalcy of an acceptable teenager's life. Going to this school was one of the best things my parents could have ever done. However, the year passed quickly, and with tears bursting down my face, my mom and I pulled away from the school. Summer vacation had begun, and it was time for me to go home. I pulled away from the school feeling stronger, self-aware, and spiritually in tune with God with a much clearer path.

The saying "All good things must come to an end" came true. One week home, all good! Two weeks home? Bad! How I got messed up with him again, I don't even know. My resolve did not even last two full weeks. So off to the school I went to live with my principal and his wife.

This guy's hold on me was stronger than before, and this time he did not stay away. It did not take long before the principal's wife discerned what was happening, and she came to me suggesting we fast for one day and pray that I would never see this man again. I agreed.

On this particular day, we were leaving to go visit a Bible camp and spend time with some friends. I was upstairs getting ready when I saw a piece of Juicy Fruit gum in my purse. I remember thinking, "If I could just taste the juice of the gum." I was so hungry. However, when I reached for it, I literally heard the audible voice of God speak and say, "No, Sonia." *This voice was the calmest, kindest voice I had ever heard, yet at the same time full of authority.* I obeyed!

When we arrived at the camp, I was immediately approached by my principal, who told me this guy was here. My principal had a friend with him who had an over-the-top, inflated ego that basically just wanted to punch this guy's lights out. I was whirling with emotions. The one thought that stood out was, "Lord, we are fasting and praying I will never see him again; he is here, and I am going to see him." The wisdom of my principal was amazing. I remember him saying, "I promised your parents I would never leave you alone with this man." Really? What? You talked to my parents? Also, he said, "He [this man] gave me a letter for you to read. Do you want it, or would you like me to destroy it?" "Destroy it," I said. "Now," he said, "would you like to talk with him?" Yes! So we walked to a tree where he stood. My principal sat on one side of the tree, and we sat on the other side.

I can't tell you a single word said between us; however, I do remember feeling "icky." When he left, my principal's wife and I got back in the car and drove home. I about died when I saw the guy in the distance hitchhiking, so I ducked my head down. I did not sit back up until I was told we were far enough past him and it was safe.

Even though my parents lived right next door to his house, I have never seen this guy since that day, the day of the fast. And I know I will NEVER see him again! The "stronghold" was broken!

> *Finally, be strong in the Lord and His mighty power. Put on the full armor of God so that you can take your stand against the devil's schemes. For our struggle is not against flesh and blood, but against the rulers, against the authorities, against the powers of this dark world and against the spiritual forces of evil in the Heavenly realms.*
>
> —Ephesians 6:10-12

Honoring Your Parents

Children obey your parents in the Lord, for this is right. Honor your father and mother which is the first commandment with a promise ... that it may go well with you and that you may enjoy long life on the earth.

—Ephesians 6:1-3

As a teenager I did not have much value or respect for my parents. We collided on many issues. I was always disappointed with them, and their authority curled my lip in disgust. I simply did not need them, nor did I have any understanding of their love or sacrifices. I was pretty much wrapped up in my own world of desires. I was right; they were wrong, and they just did not understand me.

I found myself in first-period Bible class listening intently as the teacher went off the topic and began talking about honoring and respecting your parents. There was a conduit that carried the Holy Spirit's words from her mouth to my soul. As she spoke, all the students dissipated or faded to the outer shadows of the classroom, like in the movies where in the final scene the couple dances on the floor with only the spotlight revealing their love. And so it was that particular morning with the Holy Spirit piercing my soul, shedding His truths deep into my heart.

I wish I could remember all that she said that day. It seemed as though she talked for hours with me mesmerized and in a trance, listening to every word she spoke. I do remember her saying, "Your parents are God-given, and He requires your respect to them. When you go home, it is their home; it is their house, and regardless of how you feel toward them, you are required to honor and obey them."

Now, I know this is nothing new; however, when words are spoken with the Holy Spirit's enlightenment, it opens the heart to understanding, acceptance, and change. And that is what happened that morning in first-period class.

Even though I had a lot of healing ahead of me and issues that needed solving, at least from that day forward the foundation was laid for this to take place. I have never viewed my parents the same way since. The God of the universe came down that morning and took time to place in my heart a wonderful new perspective that forevermore changed my outlook toward my God-given parents! Again, when the Holy Spirit speaks to the soul of man, the soul of man is forever changed.

Children, obey your parents in everything, for this pleases the Lord.

—Colossians 3:20

The Glory of God

Then Moses said, "Now show me your glory. And the Lord said, "I will cause all my goodness to pass in front of you, and I will proclaim my name, the Lord, in your presence. I will have mercy on whom I will have mercy and I will have compassion on whom I will have compassion. But, he said, you cannot see my face, for no one may see me and live. Then the Lord said, "There is a place near me where you may stand on a rock. When my glory passes by, I will put you in a cleft in the rock and cover you with my hand until I have passed by. Then I will remove my hand and you will see my back; but my face must not be seen.

—Exodus 33:18-23

I was sitting in one of many chapel services required of me while attending a small private Bible school. In this particular service, we had a guest speaker. The only thing I remember of the sermon that day was he challenged us students to spend time daily and privately seeking God. He even made a recommendation: "You guys have an hour lunch, so take half of it and eat and the other half to find a quiet place to seek the Lord in prayer and Bible reading."

Even though I was raised in the church, I really had no understanding of a relationship with Jesus Christ. I had knowledge of Jesus but not a personal relationship, nor did I know it could exist. So when I took the challenge of seeking God, I had no preconditioned idea of what would transpire.

I went to my dormitory room, pulled the shades down, locked the door, and opened my Bible. It was magical! The Bible became alive! The characters of the stories were as though I was there in the midst of them all. Jesus's parables pierced my soul, and I found myself, for the first time, on my knees worshipping God, praising God, thanking God, and adoring Him. Hear me, because this is probably one of the most amazing times of my life. When I even come close to not believing or should I ever doubt that God exists or Jesus Christ is the atonement of sin, I come back to this: God's glory used to come into my dormitory room so much and so powerfully that I used to pray, "God, don't come any closer because I cannot contain your glory." It was profound! God exists! His love for man— for you, for me—is not anything I can put into words.

I remember one time leaving my room and walking out into the lounge area when a guy friend stopped me and asked what I was doing in my room every lunch hour. When I asked why, he said, "Because when you come out, you are glowing." WOW! I was glowing?

I want to stop here a minute and say this about prayer. It is not a "one, two, three" step to follow, nor is it a concrete do "this" and "this" will always happen. It is just my experience. It has only been during my praise and worship time that the joy and glory of God is revealed. We seem to think, or at least I did, that prayer is only a time of confessing our sins, asking for help, or giving and reminding God of our list of needs. Of course, there are those needed prayers and definitely a time for those prayers. However, I am a firm believer that more should be on our knees bowed before the throne of God, worshipping Him as the Holy Spirit leads, entering His presence by the way of the cross, the blood of our savior Jesus Christ.

Have you ever come before the throne of God and lay in the spirit prostrate and kissed His feet because of the mercy He has shown you? Have you ever in the spirit rested your face on His knee and allowed His love to heal you of life's overwhelming concerns? Have you ever danced before his throne in the joy of your salvation and for knowing your security in eternity? I have, I do, and it is in those times that God speaks to me and swells my heart with His joy and glory.

> *When Moses came down from Mount Sinai with the two tablets of the Testimony in his hands, he was not aware that his face was radiant because he had spoken with the Lord.*
>
> —Exodus 34:29

God's Voice

The voice of the Lord is powerful; the voice of the Lord is majestic.
—Psalm 29:4-5

I have kept a book within arms' reach ever since I read it many years ago. It is a true story of a Muslim woman's conversion to Christianity, *I Dared to Call Him Father*. I was astonished to read her words describing the audible voice of God to be almost identical to my description of God's voice. This Muslim woman was reading the Koran and the Bible at the same time. She states she read the Koran out of duty but was drawn out of passion to read the Bible. It was at her sweet confession of sin and her acceptance of Jesus Christ as the atonement of her sins that she heard the voice of God. In her need to know, she held the Koran up in one hand and the Bible in the other hand, and she asked God, "Which, Father? Which one is Your Book?" And God spoke, "In which book do you meet Me as your Father?"

This voice she describes was **fresh, full of kindest, yet at the same time full of authority.** She further says, "It was the most remarkable thing; nothing like it had ever occurred in my life in quite this way. For I heard a voice inside my being, a voice that spoke to me as clearly as if I were repeating words in my inner mind."

Now, I just have to say, is not it just like God to have such a perfect answer? God's answer astonishes me just as much as someone else's almost identical description of God's voice. God is so respectful of man. Always allowing free choice/will. He just simply asked a question, allowing this woman to distinguish the correct answer.

When I first heard God's voice, it was during the time I attended a private Bible school. During our two-week Christmas break, about thirty talented singers would travel the northern states and sing at churches. This was an amazing time with great friends and a bonding that still holds many of us together today.

We traveled by way of a Greyhound bus. It was at one of its many rest stops that I heard the voice of God. I was bebopping out of the store on my way back to the bus, singing some praise song in my head, when from out of nowhere God spoke and said, "Go tell her I love her." God's voice, as stated above, was the ***calmest, kindest voice I ever heard, yet at the same time full of authority***.

When I looked up, I saw a lady pumping gas into her car. Several people stood in that direction, but I knew it was her. Now I am sorrowfully sad to say and have regretted my whole life that I did not go. Why? I don't know! I had a moment of rationalization and moved on. I have prayed for that woman my whole life. Why all-knowing God asked me to tell her He loved her, knowing I would not, is beyond me. I am convinced, though, I am the one who truly missed out on something spectacular that day. God loved that woman, and He found a way to her without my help. I am the one who missed the blessing that day!

The Voice of the Lord is majestic.

—Psalm 29:4

The Joke

Our mouths were filled with laughter (there is a time to laugh, dance and be joyful).

—Psalm 126:2

I love a good joke. Laughter is so good for the soul; endorphins are released, your spirit flies, and healing can take place for the downcast person. Laughing is just good! I have often said a successful night out with friends is one where a couple of good deep-belly, tear-producing, throw-your-hands-over-your-face, oh-my-goodness-stop-or-else laughter happens.

I was standing with a small group of people when a professor started in telling a joke. As usual my eyes lit up. "Oh, good, let the fun begin!" As the professor was setting up the joke, I was anticipating the punch line and getting ready for a hearty laugh. However, I will never forget what happened that day. When the punch line was finally delivered, my reaction to laugh was beaten out by the reaction of the Holy Spirit. I did not get a chance to laugh, for the Spirit of God jumped out ahead of me and responded with hurt. I felt my whole body involuntarily consumed by God's disappointment. It was as though I was a third party standing by, watching a split-second interaction between God and this professor. I saw the professor see God's reaction through me. I remember thinking, "But, Lord, it was relatively a clean joke." I walked away in a stunned daze, thinking, "Boy, have I ever missed the mark if that offended the Holy Spirit."

I have often wondered why this happened. I have considered maybe God needed to speak to this man, for he saw God's reaction. I have often reflected on Jesus's words, "Be Holy as I am Holy." But more often I think this happened because Jesus wants a personal interactive relationship with us, and even in this "relatively clean joke" it grieved Him. We are, I am, the temple of the living God, and what I do, what I hear, what I say, and where I go should demonstrate the Holy Spirit living within me.

So now when I hear a joke being told, I think differently. Oh, I still enjoy a good laugh, but now when the joke is being set up and the punch line hangs in the distance, my anticipation to laugh is always coupled with "I wonder who is going to respond first, me or the Holy Spirit."

> *Don't you know that you yourselves are God's temple and that God's Spirit lives in you?*
> —1 Corinthians 3:16

My Angel

Are not all angels ministering spirits sent to serve those who will inherit salvation?

—Hebrews 1:14

At nineteen years old I lay in a hospital bed in labor. I was only four or five months along, so I knew upon delivery the baby would not live. The labor pains were unbearable. My husband at the time was nowhere to be found; he went home, I guess, to sleep. I don't remember how I got left by myself during such a critical time; where were my mom, my sister, a friend, my mother-in-law, someone, anyone? Even the nurses came in sparingly to check my progress. I just lay there curled up on my side, hanging on to those metal side railings for dear life with each and every contraction.

During one of my contractions, I remember looking up just in time to see my angel walk by. He caught eyes with me, took two steps back, and walked into my room. He gently pried my hands loose from the metal railings and said, "Here, take my hands and squeeze as tight as you need to." My angel looked like Grizzly Adams dressed in white, wearing a lab jacket. He stayed just long enough. It was a little boy, and I named him Michael (never told anyone this). I know he (and one other baby I lost) are safe in Heaven. How nice for them to be forever in the presence of God. I don't know what Heaven will be like as far as wanting to do anything but adore God, but rest assured, when the time comes, my two babies will be the first ones I seek out. I am so very excited to meet them.

I will always remember this man and the kindness he showed to a young girl. With no doubt, I am positive I squeezed his hands really hard! His gentleness will always be remembered, and even though he literally was not an angel, I saw his wings that night.

For he will command his angels concerning you to guard you in all your ways! They will lift you up in their hand.

—Psalm 91:11

Stirring of Words

For the word of God is living and active. Sharper than any dou-
ble-edged sword, it penetrates even to dividing soul and spirit, joints
and marrow; it judges the thoughts and attitudes of the heart.
                                        —Hebrews 4:12

God is so far above and beyond what we think or can imagine. God
speaks to us through the Bible, His written word. Foremost, we
should seek to know Him through reading the Bible, for answers are
found; healing is given; direction to life is revealed; understanding,
truth, and wisdom are imparted; and love is shown.

However, God chose another form of communicating one day.
I was hanging out in my apartment with my son when my good
friend stopped by with her guy friend. We got into a deep stimulat-
ing discussion when the young man began complaining and ques-
tioning God's ways. As he spoke, I began having words stir in my
spirit. Not in my mind, but in my spirit. I had this wrestling of
words deep in my soul, and I was extremely disturbed over what
this guy was saying. I know my head was not physically shaking
back and forth as if to say, "No, no," but inwardly it was. When it
was clear he was done complaining, I opened my mouth to speak,
and all of a sudden there was this unexpected flow of words that just
poured out of my mouth. With no effort from myself, these words
flowed clear, unbroken, with authority and power. The words came
from my spirit and not from my mind. I saw this young man spellbound. It was only when my friend said, "Preach it, Sonia," that my

gaze turned from him to her and back again to him, and the words were gone.

I don't even remember what was said. But I will always remember the power of the words spoken through me that day. Without a second of doubt, I know this young man was changed from that moment forward, for when God reaches down (in any form He chooses) and touches a man's soul, that soul from that moment forward is forever changed.

> *As the Heavens are higher than the earth, so are my ways higher than your ways and my thoughts than your thoughts.*
> —Isaiah 55:9

I Put You Together in Your Mother's Womb

For you created my inmost being; you knit me together in my mother's womb.

—Psalm 139:13

Have you ever been in a place or a time in your life that you felt so insignificant? Completely of no value to a soul? That if you fell off the face of the earth, no one would have noticed? Well, I have! It was a dark time. At age twenty-three, I was a single parent of a three-year-old son. I was caught between being single but responsible for a child and tied down but free. Many nights I spent alone believing I was never thought of by any given person. The show *The Love Boat* and a bowl of popcorn had become my best friends.

This insignificance was of the soul; I had no self-worth. When viewing other people, they all outshone me in every way! This brought me to my knees before God many nights. I remember crying before His throne wondering why He ever made me. I thought back over my life and just came up short of any value, with nothing significant to offer. I had no skills, talents, or intelligence, and now I felt lonely and unloved.

It was at this time a wonderful, sweet injection by the Holy Spirit changed my life forever. It was at this time the Spirit of God spoke to my heart and called me by name and said, ***"How dare you call what I made insignificant."*** In that moment, God showed me His love and gave me the understanding of this love. As I stayed on my knees and soaked in His revealing love, it became the vantage point of my existence. Any self-worthlessness took back seat to knowing God loved me. Any failed ambitions, lack of direction or purpose became powerless, knowing God had me in His sight. This understanding was the catalyst to my healing. I got up from my knees that night, changed. His love swelled my heart. His acceptance of me flooded my eyes with tears. The God who loved me, the God who made my every part, who designed me and knew me from all of time was now my ambition.

Did I struggle after this in keeping my focus on God's love for me? Yes and no. Day-to-day living can really cause havoc on life. Daily grind and responsibility can quickly take our focus off the Lord. But ever since God challenged me and called me out on His creation—me—the foundation of my heart has never been the same. Resting in His love, His acceptance, and knowing my value in Him have kept me from the trap of self-worthlessness. Again, when the Holy Spirit changes the heart, the heart is forever changed. ***God loves me,*** and even better, ***God likes me***. I sit here with a big smile on my face and joy in my heart because the God of the universe, the God of creation, the God of **ALL** loves/likes me! It just does not get any sweeter than that!

> *I praise you because I am fearfully and wonderfully made; your works are wonderful, I know that full well. My frame was not hidden from you when I was made in the secret place. When I was woven together in the depths of the earth, your eyes saw my unformed body. All the days ordained for me were written in your book before one of them came to be.*
>
> —Psalm 139:14-16

God Outside the Box

He answered, "Haven't you read what David did when he and his companions were hungry? He entered the house of God, and he and his companions ate the consecrated bread—which was not lawful for them to do, but only for the priests."

—Matthew 11:3

Oh my goodness, God is God and can do what He wants. Who are we to put Him in a box of our upbringing? With good motives and conviction of their beliefs, our parents, church leaders, and even schoolteachers taught many things—rights and wrongs, work ethics, accountability, responsibility, and interpretation of Holy Scripture. Which leads me to this experience:

I have always wanted to go to cosmetology school; after many failed attempts, I checked into going one more time. I had three small children and two stepchildren. I worked full-time and was in a huge remodel of our home. Life was over-the-top stressful. However, I found a community college about forty-five minutes away, and it was afford-able. The cosmetology program required five days a week, eight hours a day for one year, forcing me to quit my job. But I was absolutely in no position of not bringing in money for the household expenses. So at age thirty-seven, I humbled myself from being a medical secretary to waiting tables at night. For those of you who have never waited tables or have forgotten what it is like, let me remind you: it is a "young" person's show! Going back to waiting tables later in life is just not that pretty; everyone is young, full of drama, and "know-it-all."

After an interview with a relatively nice local chain restaurant, I was driving home feeling really discouraged when I passed a little small hole-in-the-wall local bar/club restaurant, and the Lord spoke to my heart and said, "Apply." What? Apply? Serve Alcohol? As I was rationalizing with the Lord, I felt this magnetic tug pulling me toward the place, so I pulled in, walked inside, applied, and was hired on the spot.

With alcohol abuse in my family, we were brought up without any in our home. I have never seen an alcoholic drink in my father's hand, but I remember my mother telling me the story that my dad did drink heavily when we kids were young. She told me she was at her end with his behavior and decided if that was his choice for the family, then it would be her choice as well. So she told him, "When you stop and buy your beer for the night, make sure whatever amount you buy for yourself, you buy that same amount for me." Like I said, I have never seen a drink in my dad's hand. Added to this, I grew up with the church teaching alcohol was sinful. I grew up without it in the home, and to this day there are no activities within my parents' home that include alcohol.

Our Lord is amazing! It was totally wild to my thought process that the LORD would have me apply in a bar/club/restaurant to serve drinks. I was so green, so to be hired was truly an act of God. I completely had no understanding of wine, beer, liquor, or mixed drinks. I am sure I blew the bartender's mind when "calling out my drink orders." But it was a small local club; it reminded me of the sitcom *Cheers*. It was an older, mature wait staff. We had our own nightly sections of responsibility, but we put all the tips we made in a common container, and it was split at the end of the night. This took the tension off. We generally helped each other out; no one seemed to be out for themselves, and we worked as a team. Genius of the Lord to put me in such a wonderful workplace—just perfect!

The hours I put in between school and work were probably around seventy-five a week. I would make it to school by 8:00 a.m., and at 4:30 p.m., I would change into my work clothes to be at work by 5:15 p.m. My day ended somewhere between midnight and 3:00 a.m.

Before actually committing to this schedule, I told my mother about it, and I will always remember her words, for they surged me with power: "You can do anything for one year." And she was right!

I say all this to say that God knew right where I needed to be. And even though I knew God spoke and said, "Apply," it was totally outside the box of my upbringing.

I know there is black and white and a right-and-wrong message of the Bible. There are uncompromising scriptures that can never be justified. However, let us be very wise and nonjudgmental of our God, who can and will operate outside the BOX of our upbringing! Without question, the God who knows me said, "Apply."

> *If you had known what these words mean "I desire mercy, not sacrifice," you would not have condemned the innocent. For the Son of Man is Lord of the Sabbath.*
>
> —Matthew 11:7-8

The Promised Clientele

*Now faith is being sure of what we hope for and certain of what
we do not see.*

—Hebrews 11:1

Halfway through my cosmetology education, I remember being
awakened to the words I was saying: "Thank you, God, for my clientele." My forty-five-minute drive to school was my time of prayer
and meditation, and somewhere along the way God gave me a
calm knowing/faith that He would bring me a clientele right out of
school. I knew it! I just had this overwhelming gratitude of "thank
you, Lord!"

Just before graduating, I started searching for a salon in which
to work. I had checked out many different ones, but it was when I
walked into this one particular salon that I knew I was home. This
salon was a lease salon, which meant you worked for yourself, bought
your own supplies, and paid a weekly fee/rent for your space. I had
NO clientele, which equates to NO income! My sister, who had been
doing hair for some time, gave me a very nice pair of scissors, and
the owner of the salon, on her own accord, vouched for me, which
allowed me to buy my supplies on credit.

And just like God said, from day one, I have never sat, unheard
of straight out of school. People came from all directions to get their
hair done. I remember thinking the second week of work that I
needed two of me. At one point, a nail technician approached me
and said, "I have been in the salon business for over thirty years,

36

and I have never seen this happen to a single hairstylist right out of school."

Going to cosmetology school was never about the money. In fact, I never knew you could make such a good living doing hair. Desiring to be a hairstylist has always been about the people I believed God would bring to me; doing hair was a platform to share Christ in whatever capacity I could. There have been many times I actually stood amazed at the power of God speaking through me: the clarity of thought and the eloquence of words or wisdom that came from God. I saw it in the clients' eyes when it happened. Each time God spoke his heart through me, I would kind of giggle and smile inwardly, thanking God for the opportunity to be used. I stood even more amazed at the people God brought into my life who encouraged me and allowed God to speak through them to me. I have been so blessed by my clients. I have always viewed every single person who walked through my door and whoever sat in my chair as brought by God. So when I asked the question, "What are we doing with your hair today?" I was simultaneously asking, "God, what are we doing with this soul today?"

I have had so many wonderful interactions with my clients over the years, but one man in particular stands out. His demeanor was gentle, kind, and humble, and he always came in with a genuine smile. From day one, the Lord gave me the responsibility to pray for him. I always looked for the opportunity to present Christ, but it never opened up. But God is faithful, and after ten long years of waiting and praying, it finally happened. During his haircut appointment, our conversation led to death, afterlife, and eventually to each other's faith. During this conversation, piece by piece the whole plan of salvation unfolded. I was so excited and amazed how perfectly it went, naturally and effortlessly, just the way he needed to hear it and right on God's long ten-year timetable. Although he did not accept Christ that day, I knew the Holy Spirit planted a seed deep in his soul for someone else to water and nurture. He walked out that day with me knowing my part was fulfilled.

My prayer for you, for me, is that we would be faithful in the mission field before us every day. At work; at home; to our children, parents, spouse, grandkids; to the clerk or bagger; the car in front of us; or the person on the other end of the phone—that we would demonstrate the love, the grace, and the mercy we have received from Christ. That we would remember to be kind, to be forgiving, to lift up, to encourage, to help, to extend, to be the mouth, hands, and feet of Christ while we walk this earth.

With a heart of extreme gratitude, I thank God for every person who has ever sat in my chair; so many have richly blessed me, and I know with every ounce of my being that if you have ever sat in my chair, God put you there.

And without faith it is impossible to please God, because anyone who comes to him must believe that he exists and that he rewards those who earnestly seek him.

—Hebrews 11:6

Don't Be an Island

Be devoted to one another in brotherly love.
—Romans 12:10

I learned early in life that we all "put our pants on one leg at a time."
That is why I am an open book when it comes to sharing my life. I
have seen the most distressed person drop their shoulders and see their
face relax with acceptance when I bared my soul. You can almost hear
them say, "Really?" "I am okay?" "I am normal?" especially when it
brings light on their hidden darkness. We are all so very much alike,
and we are not meant to be "an island unto ourselves." My demons
may not be yours, my issues may not mimic yours exactly, but none-
theless, what you do suppress and hold within would probably help
someone just like yourself if you opened up and realized we are all
just trying to do our best with what we know.

With the above stated, I am not suggesting we brag about our
"sins" or failures. In fact, in the midst of acting out against God, I
hide them. Not until I find repentance and forgiveness do I want to
share. It is with great humility and thankfulness of God's grace and
mercy that I open up and let you see my inner self.

Let me give you an example: I am a hairstylist, privileged to
many conversations, and I have heard just about everything. Even
if I don't want to hear them, I have no choice, for I am held "captive" by you during our visits as you are by me. I had a lady sitting
in my chair one day struggling with an issue. Without her saying it,
I knew what it was because she danced around it the whole time,

saying everything but that nasty embarrassing word. So I said it for her, "Just so you know, I filed *bankruptcy*." Her eyes shot up big as saucers! I continued on with my story, acting as though I had no clue this was her situation. When I was done, tears came to her eyes, and she barely whispered the words, but she did: "I just filed bankruptcy." Anyone who has ever sat in some recovery/addiction class knows the drill. It is very difficult to stand up and introduce yourself and admit your addiction due to the feelings of failure, defeat, and shame, and it is no different in sharing failure in your finances:

> Hi, my name is _____, and I am a recovering JFB (Just Filed Bankruptcy).

And just like that, healing sets in! I think it is one of Satan's biggest weapon against us—making us think we are the only person who "did" or "thought" or even "felt" anything unimaginable, so we will hide our shame instead of confessing it and finding healing. Kind of like when Adam and Eve sinned and they hid themselves from God. If Satan can keep us separated from our Maker, we will be ineffective for His Kingdom.

Another example: I had an out-of-control, over-the-top teenage son. Actually it began somewhere in fifth grade. He just woke up one day and was a different kid; it lasted a very, VERY long time. I remember thinking when he left at night (usually under GREAT distress) that if he got into a car accident and died, it would be a welcomed relief. In hindsight, these are absolutely horrific thoughts! At the time I thought them, I slammed my hands over my ears. I can hardly type the words even today. I **LOVE** my son! However, I was emotionally maxed out with no relief in sight.

Now, I had a lady sitting in my chair getting her hair done, explaining to me the turmoil of her son. It was apparent the heartache she suffered. I could see the pain she carried. I began thinking, "Oh goodness, could I tell her the thoughts I had? Would she judge me harshly, a mother wishing her son dead? Surely, no sound, good, loving mother would ever think such a thing. Sonia, these are only your thoughts. How could anyone else ever think of such a thing?" I never spoke the words out loud. I never told anyone these thoughts, for shame gripped me! However, I wanted to help her, so I began telling her some of my struggles I had with my son. And then, with an extreme exhale of complete vulnerability, I said, "I used to think if my son died in a car accident, it would have been okay with me because I would have relief." After I exhaled these terrifying thoughts, the most shocking thing happened; she confessed the *exact same thoughts*. Oh my gosh. I was spellbound! No way! Someone else thought the same thoughts! You can only guess what happened next: MY HEALING BEGAN. She felt better, and her healing began as well! I was no longer an island unto myself! I was normal! I hid those bad, horrible feelings forever, thinking what a monster of a mother I was!

I realize we are all wired up just a little differently. I am an extrovert, a people person, helper, and pleaser by nature, so it is easy for me to open up. However, there are many who are a little bit more private and reserved, and it would be extremely difficult to share the most private areas of their lives. If you discover you are one who finds it difficult to share your island secrets, then I would encourage you to share them with Christ. I pray you find comfort in His forgiveness and acceptance in His grace and mercy, for He says, "Come unto me all you who are weary and burdened, and I will give you rest."

Carry each other's burdens, and in this way you will fulfill the law of Christ.

—Galatians 6:2

The Closet Smoker

Three times I pleaded with the Lord to take it away from me. But he said to me my grace is sufficient for you, for my power is made perfect in weakness.

—2 Corinthians 12:8-9

So here is one of those times in my life that I strayed from God. Can you believe at age thirty-one I became a closet smoker? Just to be clear, do I think smoking is a "sin"? No, I don't unless God said NO. So anything can become sin when God says no and you choose not to obey.

I knew God was disappointed in my actions. I was ashamed and hence became a closet smoker. Amazing, right? A Christian since I was seventeen with many amazing experiences and yet still stubborn enough to choose my own way. I shake my head even as I write these words. After a while sin produces a separation from the flow of God's spirit, and before long I was out of touch with God altogether and frankly going my own way.

There would be times I craved a cigarette so badly, and with no place to hide, I would smoke around those I really did not want to smoke around. I knew I was not glorifying God, but the need for a cigarette replaced my shame. I rode this fence for a long time. Reason? One word: addiction. But the Holy Spirit's conviction never left my side.

I want to stop here and tell a side story: I attended a church and became good friends with the pastor and his wife because I was their hairstylist. During one of the salon visits, the pastor told me about this elderly godly woman whom he highly respected. He suggested if I ever needed to talk to someone, he would recommend her.

Sometime later, she became my client, and so began our relationship as hairstylist and client/friend. During one of my many attempts to quit smoking, she came in to get her hair done. I was on day three of not smoking, and I was struggling. So with the seed planted from my pastor that she was a "godly" woman and one he recommended I talk with, I began pouring out my frustrations, failures, and guilt regarding smoking. She said many things that day, but the most stunning and shocking of all was, "Girl, go have yourself a cigarette. There is nothing wrong with that." What? Had I heard wrong from God? All of a sudden I felt like a pin ball just shot out of its socket, uncontrollably bouncing off every emotional obstacle there was. My rationalization kicked in, my justification kicked in, and I was now weakened in my resolve; I was now single-focused—to smoke a cigarette.

My friend went on to explain her viewpoint; however, I don't remember a single word, for the lack of nicotine had now hit its all-time high. All I wanted was to hurry and get her hair done and find a cigarette. I mean, goodness, a "godly" woman gave me permission to smoke! (I will come back to this story.)

I tried quitting so many times. I hated that I was not obeying God. I would pray and get my resolve, only to lose it an hour later. I had so many noble reasons to stop. Goodness, what a poor example to my children. I exercised every day and preached clean eating. However, nothing was more disturbing to me than not walking in God's glory and peace.

I prayed often for God's power to help me quit. I would often remind Him of my true heart. I really desired to bring him glory with my obedience. I desired to be a woman after His own heart like King David. I remember praying one day and saying I did not care what quitting meant even if I got fat (huge concern for those who smoke to stay skinny). All I cared about was having fellowship with the Lord. I wanted to be in His glory and have His peace back in my heart.

It was soon after this prayer that the Lord spoke to me. Why now after many prayer sessions? I don't know! But once again, I was in prayer, hashing over my failure. I told Him I just did not have the discipline to stop smoking AND I was defeated. And then God whispered these sweet healing words to my heart, "Where you are weak, I am strong." He spoke and said, "You don't have the discipline you need, but I do, and all you have to do is ask for it." And there you have it! I have NEVER picked up another cigarette from that day forward. When the craving hit, I opened my mouth in prayer, and before the word "discipline" was even completely spoken, the Lord's discipline surged into my body. It took about three months of me calling on the Lord's discipline, and every time the Lord was faithful!

Several years after this healing, there were maybe two or three times I found myself ever so slightly craving a cigarette; Satan tried, but I quickly called on God's discipline, and just like before, God's surge of power and strength went through me. Now, today, I just simply thank God that I am smoke-free. I thank God all the time He opened my eyes to what my weakness was and showed me my answer.

So if you have an addiction or a hang-up, I think the best place to start is at the foot of the cross, confessing even the simplest of need. If you find you have no peace or joy with your salvation, then rewind every step until you get to the place of your resistance with God and then from that place plead His answers for your healing. God desires, God demands obedience.

Now back to the "elderly godly lady." We need to be so careful with what we say to one another. I am sure this lady's advice was pure of heart. I am sure she meant well. I believe she is a woman who loves the Lord. I also believe, for her, smoking is not an issue in serving the Lord. But she was a "stumbling block" to me that day.

I smoked that cigarette, and once again the glory of God was gone. God's peace left my heart. I was depressed and sad with once again, disobeying my Lord.

> *I am fully convinced that no food is unclean in itself. But if anyone regards something as unclean, then for him it is unclean.*
> —Romans 14:14

We All Enter Eternity Equal

What good will it be for a man if he gains the whole world, yet forfeits his soul? Or what can a man give in exchange for his soul?
—Matthew 16:26

Why some are born to privilege and others are not will only be understood in Heaven. However, from earth to eternity, the rich and the poor will enter Heaven in one way—through the recognition of sin and the need of the Savior Jesus. I believe the Bible teaches that the very best person here on earth falls completely short of any holiness to merit their own entry before God. Likewise, the worst criminal that you can possibly think of will stand in Heaven upon acceptance of Jesus Christ as the atonement for their sin.

I don't pretend to even come close to knowing the fate of a person's soul. However, I can't help but think of the great artists and singers Michael Jackson or Elvis (I loved Elvis). I think of contributing and influential people who changed the course of action, such as President Abraham Lincoln or scientists such as Albert Einstein and Benjamin Franklin. What about the talented and incredible artists Michelangelo and Leonardo Da Vinci? We have history full of amazing poets, dancers, athletes, physicians, philosophers, astronomers, and let's not forget about the sacrificial and loving Mother Teresa. Goodness, the list can go on and on. The clerk you met today, your boss, the person in church next to you, your child or spouse, a parent, friend, sister, brother, aunts, and uncles—there are souls everywhere, and they are headed somewhere for all of eternity. When you take your last breath here on earth, no matter your talent, accomplishments, trophies, wealth, or education, eternity starts.

It grieves me to hear people say they will chance standing before God based on knowing he is a loving and compassionate God. The word "chance" screams out to me! When your life hangs in the "balance" for eternity, you are going to "chance" it? Living in the dispensational age of mercy and grace, it is easy to forget that God set a plan in place that will never change. His Kingdom will never be destroyed and His dominion will never end. He is God, and He is sending His Son back; He will judge the hearts of man. His questions to every single person will be, "Do you know my Son? Is he your Lord and Savior? Did you believe in the blood of the Lamb that takes away sin?" With each individual answer, the separation between good and evil will occur.

All this sounds pretty harsh, I know, but I did not say it. God did! However, I believe it. I further believe God loves man and pleads with man to see his provision. God provides a way through Christ to escape this judgment. His provision to you is not to "chance" your placement in eternity but that you would "know" your placement.

And Jesus said, I am the way and the truth and the life. No one comes to the Father except through me.
—John 14:6

For God so loved the world that he gave his one and only Son, that whoever believes in him shall nor perish but have eternal life.
—John 3:16

When the Son of Man comes in his glory, and all the angels with him, he will sit on his throne in the Heavenly glory. All the nations will be gathered before him, and he will separate the people one from another as a shepherd separates the sheep from the goats. He will put the sheep on his right and the goats on his left.
—Matthew 25:31-33

The God of Grace and Mercy

But God demonstrates his love for us in this: while we were still sinners Christ died for us.

—Romans 5:8

Can you even begin to fathom or comprehend the salvation of your soul? I gave my life to the Lord around seventeen years of age. I do not have any profound memory such as a date or time of day, but I know I was a teenager. I believe I have always had some understanding of God, Jesus, and the Holy Spirit as my mom took us kids to church.

Now, I know there are two distinct interpretations of the Bible regarding salvation: one is that once saved, always saved, and the other belief is you can lose your salvation. Since I am not writing a book on theology, I am just going to say I believe the Bible supports the theory that once saved, always saved, and this is where God's grace and mercy blows me away. I am brought to my knees before the throne of God worshiping Him and praising Him because even though I have been saved since seventeen and sealed with the Holy Spirit, I have not been the best student. At age fifty-two, there is a lot of "hindsight" revealing just that. I, like Paul, proclaim loudly I am a sinner of all sinners. I am extremely stubborn and selfish, and I simply have gone my own way many times. I, like Paul, also have said many times, "The good that I want to do, I don't; and the bad I don't want to do, I do." Again, I thank God for his love. Thank you, Jesus, for your sacrifice! Thank you, Holy Spirit, for convicting me and holding me accountable.

God, as the Bible states, is all-knowing! Think about that! I have had so many amazing injections of God's power throughout my life. Yet with Him knowing I would walk away, rebel, do it my way, "sin" at different times in my life, it did not stop Him from revealing Himself to me. It did not stop His love! God sealed my soul by way of the cross, placing the Holy Spirit in me for all eternity, knowing I would actively sin against him. What a LOVE! That is grace and mercy revealed at its finest! "God, have mercy upon me and my family. Show yourself to us that we will be saved."

For God so loved the world that he gave his one and only Son, that whoever believes in him shall not perish but have eternal life.
—John 3:16

Poem

After meditating one day in prayer and worshipping God, He gave me a vision of Jesus on the cross, and afterward I wrote this poem:

My Savior

I saw my Savior today.
I saw him as the only way.
With thorns on his head
I saw the wounds on his back that bled.
I wanted to run to him!
I ached with something to say
But what could I say ...
Except there is no other way!
I was so helpless as I stood there and cried.
And as my Savior looked at me with loved-filled eyes
I laid my head low
And as I wept, all I could say was
Thank you
Thank you
My Savior, thank you ... There is just no other way.

Surely he took up our infirmities and carried our sorrows, yet we considered him stricken by God, smitten by him, and afflicted. But he was pierced for our transgressions, he was crushed for our iniquities; the punishment that brought us peace was upon him. And by his wounds we are healed.

—Isaiah 53:4-5

Save the Guppies

Then Jesus came to them and said, "All authority in Heaven and on earth has been given to me. Therefore go and make disciples of all nations, baptizing them in the name of the Father and of the Son and of the Holy Spirit, and teaching them to obey everything I have commanded you. And surely I am with you always, to the very end of the age.

—Matthew 28:18-20

I have always felt "called." What I mean by this is nothing seems to measure up against total submission to "God's work"; all thoughts pale in comparison. When I sit down and really contemplate life, nothing seems more important than the end result—where will you and I live for all eternity?

The call to evangelism comes to mind. But how do you become a Dwight L. Moody, Billy Graham, Charles Spurgeon, or Watchman Nee? It makes you want to question your heart and what you truly believe. Do you really have the faith and passion required? I often think of the apostle Paul and his letters to the different churches, many of which were written while in prison. It seemed he never wavered from the moment he met Jesus on the road to Damascus. I pray for that resolve.

I have always strived for that big moment! Something spectacular, you know, like "saving the whales." I am not sure I think this is so bad. Goals are important. Even over-the-top goals are good, for they keep us looking forward and make life exciting. Being driven takes us past existing to the place of "living."

However, when I really stop and think about the true meaning of life, I always come back to the love for souls. I want people to know Christ their Redeemer. "Store up for yourself treasures [souls] in Heaven." This verse and my love for God lead me to want to drop all earthly desires and totally dive headfirst (no toe-testing the waters) into the life of Jesus and the principles he taught while he walked on earth. Yup! I know, over the top! But that is me and always has been. I am a bit of a romantic and a dreamer, which has paralyzed me because, like most, I am just normal. No outrageous opportunities, no winning the lotto, no over-the-top special talent, just your everyday normal person who would love to "save the whales."

One day I was sharing this passion with my mother, and she said something that was so simple yet so profound: "Stop worrying about the whales when there are so many guppies right here in your backyard." That statement stunned me! I have always been consumed with being spectacular and getting to a place of influence. Always thinking that if I could just get myself "set up," I could serve God successfully, all the while completely missing the mission field right before me.

How exciting life can be when the proper perspective is shown. It dawned on me my "treasure to store up" is how I give my life to those God entrusted to me: foremost, my spouse, children, grandchildren, those I interact with daily, and those who play a role in my life. Please, don't misunderstand me; I believe we need to be intentional in serving God. Seeking and searching for ways to actively show our faith. However, I need to be faithful to serve and love the ones God has entrusted to me. This is my "calling."

I pray, though, and can't help but think how honored I would be if God did increase my mission field to include the whales. And if

He does, I pray that I have significantly equipped the guppies in my life to swim the seas with God as their anchor.

> *When he saw the crowds, he had compassion on them, because they were harassed and helpless, like sheep without a shepherd. Then he said to his disciples, "The harvest is plentiful but the workers are few. Ask the Lord of the harvest, therefore, to send out workers into the harvest field."*
>
> —Matthew 9:36-37

God Came Down

The following passage of scripture is one of the best visuals of God's burning love for man. I read these verses in several different ways: one, King David running from his enemies; two, God sending his son Jesus as our Redeemer; three, an interactive one-on-one personal rescue from any one of life's difficulties, which leads me to my personal vision.

Psalm 18:7-17

The earth trembled and quaked,
  and the foundations of the mountains shook;
  they trembled because he was angry!
Smoke rose from his nostrils;
  consuming fire came from his mouth,
  burning coals blazed out of it.
He parted the Heavens and came down;
  dark clouds were under his feet.
He mounted the cherubim and flew;
  he soared on the wings of the wind.
He made darkness his covering, his canopy around him …
  the dark rain clouds of the sky.
Out of the brightness of his presence clouds advanced,
  with hailstones and bolts of lightning.
The Lord thundered from Heaven;
  the voice of the Most High resounded.
He shot his arrows and scattered the enemies

great bolts of lightning and routed them.
The valleys of the sea were exposed
  and the foundations of the earth laid bare
at your rebuke, O Lord,
  at the blast of breath from your nostrils.
He reached down from on high and took hold of me;
  he drew me out of deep waters.
He rescued me from my powerful enemy,
  from my foes, who were too strong for me.

I see myself on a distant hill with enemy chariots advancing all around me. I am glancing back and forth, looking all around for an escape route with none in sight. My heart grows faint. Though inwardly my hope and my faith is in my Lord, I know my enemy is relentless in my spiritual destruction. This warrior is outwardly looking strong but inwardly feeling the child all too well. I sense my commander is telling me, "Stand still. Don't move *for your faith in my way is important for you to know at this time*." So I drop my sword and bend my knee, and with a shaking voice, I say, "I am yours. Do with me as you please. If I die, then I must die."

Then all of a sudden I look up, and I see this dark stormy cloud whirling with bolts of lightning. I notice that my enemy sees it too, but it seems to strengthen his resolve. I stand once more in faith with the presence of fear raging within. I draw my sword and raise my shield, and I cry out to my Lord, "In obedience, I will stand still and know you are God."

As you continue reading this beautiful passage of scripture, can you not just see God having enough? With purpose he stands from his throne commanding his chariot brought to him while resounding, "This is my child! Who dare raise a hand against her?" He soars from Heaven shooting his arrows and scatters my enemy. He sees me standing with my armor in place, but he knows my childlike heart and reaches down with his great big hand and rescues me. He picks me up and removes me from harm's way. He sets me in a safer pasture.

Although I am now able to rest and soak in my Lord's love, I am very aware that my enemy is still active and very much alive. I also know until I leave this earth, my enemy will find me again; however, this time I will be a little stronger in the faith because of my obedience in the previous battle.

> *Therefore put on the full armor of God, so that when the day of evil comes, you may be able to stand your ground, and after you have done everything to stand. Stand firm then, with the belt of truth buckled around your waist, with the breastplate of righteousness in place, and with your feet fitted with the readiness that comes from the gospel of peace. In addition to all this, take up the shield of faith, with which you can extinguish all the flaming arrows of the evil one. Take the helmet of salvation and the sword of the Spirit, which is the word of God. And pray in the Spirit on all occasions with all kinds of prayers and requests.*
> —Ephesians 6:13-18

My Parents' Vacation

In my distress I called to the Lord; I cried to my God for help. From his temple he heard my voice; my cry came before him, into his ears.

—Psalm 18:6

I have seen great parents whose skills in parenting are almost perfect, yet their children turn that rebellious corner and put them through hell and back. I also have seen parents who are neglectful in their parenting skills and whose children never turn that rebellious corner and grow up honoring and respecting them. It goes to show that each and every one of us has a free will. I also think the genetic bloodline runs deep. However, the blood of Christ redeems and can set free any destructive bloodline and set any "captive" free. I have three children, two of them put me through hell and back. I believe the third one just hid it better because he knew I had nothing left to offer.

After arriving home from work one evening, I found blatant significant evidence that my daughter's girlfriends had been over earlier in the day. The house was totaled! A huge pot of burnt macaroni and cheese sat on the stove (seriously, just the leftovers could have fed an army) with dirty dishes everywhere. My bathroom looked as though a fleet of girls went through it urgently getting ready on prom night. I was livid! I found my daughter in her bedroom, sitting in a daze with evidence of a recently eaten chocolate ice cream cone all over her mouth. Unable to get her attention, I stormed out!

It was not until my son came to me and pointed out the obvious that I realized she was totally wasted. "Mom," he said, "look at her eyes. She is on something." I never did see evidence of drugs with my kids. I guess when you are in the midst of it, you just can't see the abnormal behavior. Sort of like the saying, "You can't see the tree for the forest." Or better yet, when you put a frog in a pan of water and gradually turn the heat up, the frog won't know and just boils to death. Well, I did not know my daughter was boiling to death. I just figured once again my daughter had her girlfriends over while I was at work and she decided to act out. I was always ready to deal with her choices and dish out the consequences, but I missed the mark many times in seeing the true culprit—drugs! However, on this particular day, my son brought it to my attention, so I allowed her to sleep, knowing whatever needed to be dealt with would have to wait for her to be aware of her surroundings and back in the right frame of mind.

It was not until the next day when the seriousness of what happened the day before hit me. I was in my bathroom cleaning it when my daughter came in with this stunned disbelief look written all over her face, asking me why I was home and not at work. When I told her it was my normal day off, she just lost all control, falling to her knees, crying and asking, "What happened to me yesterday?" She kept shaking her head in total bewilderment, disbelief, and confusion. She had lost a whole day to drugs. She could not remember a single thing from the day before.

I can still see her face. She was lost in a world of despair, and my heart broke. When she left the bathroom, I fell to my knees, praying and asking God for direction and guidance. I pleaded with God to please help me help my daughter. I ached for His help, and then I heard His voice deep in my heart say, "Send her with your parents." I remember understanding an array of knowledge all at the same time. With that one simple statement, I understood. "She needs to see something different. She needs to know there are other places. She needs to experience a different life. She needs space and time."

My parents were leaving for a three-week canyon tour. I have not asked my parents very often for help with any one of my kids. However, I knew with confidence this was what the Lord said to do, so I simply called and asked if they would take Sarah. I stated she needed to get away. I remember my mother explaining they did not know if they could entertain her. I said, "You don't have to." My mom said, "We probably won't be doing anything that exciting for a teenager." I said, "It does not matter. I will send her with money. All I care about, Mom, is she needs to go." My mother talked with Dad and called back within minutes to say they would be leaving in the morning. I had my daughter pack her suitcase; I grabbed some money and took her to my parents' house that night.

The first couple of days were hard for my daughter because she suffered the side effects of the drug she had done. She left the next day with a really bad sore throat and woke up the following morning with a rash all over her body. My mother called with concern; however, I was sturdy as a rock and reassured my mother my daughter would be just fine. I knew God had directed the course of action, and my resolve would not be weakened.

When Sarah arrived home, she had a new spark in her eyes and a healthy smile on her face. She was excited to tell me of her many experiences. She had wonderful stories to tell me about her grandfather and grandmother, riding a horse in the canyon, and Grandpa scaring her half to death while driving down a side of a mountain. But the one experience that was emphasized and seemed to stand out the most to her was the Indian reservation and the poverty she saw.

I am moved by God's love. In a moment, God whispered into my heart the answer that set in action my daughter's healing: "Send her with your parents." This simple obedience took my daughter off the path of destruction to a path of healing and restoration. And while it did take time and suffering of past choices, she did begin taking more calculated steps that began a new path from the moment she returned from my parents' vacation.

> *I love the Lord, for he heard my voice; he heard my cry for mercy.*
> —Psalm 116:1

The Heartbreak (When We Sin)

But the thing David had done displeased the Lord.
—2 Samuel 11:1-27

I now know and believe a person can truly die of a broken heart. There are many reasons a heart can break, and I have felt my own crushed in two pieces. And here is the truth to my heartbreak: I did it to myself.

Have you ever cried so many tears that there are none left? Your tears are replaced with a painful convulsing from your gut, and you feel as though someone has their hand wrapped around your chest, squeezing it so tightly that breath is difficult to find. It is then you wish and pray God would allow you to take your last breath. You almost will it to happen. But instead, you inhale and exhale, lungs filling with air, keeping you alive. As you continue to breathe, you are faced with the knowledge that there is no relief in sight. Life, outside your will, continues.

I wish I could say my pain was outside my control, but it was not. To save "face," I wish I could say I suffered a great loss, but I did not. I wish I could say anything other than I hurt myself due to my own selfishness, and now the consequences seem unbearable.

You have to wonder how did or why does God allow these things to happen. I prayed often asking for direction. I was waiting for God's big intervention. His loud voice, clarity in spirit, maybe a prophetic word from someone. However, it did not come that way, so I continued ignoring that very "small voice," that soft, subtle knowledge. I forged forward, selfishly knowing I was ignoring the least traveled path—obedience.

I hope this is not offensive, but I sort of think of God as the ultimate gentleman. He is such the respecter of men and allows us our free will and free choices; however, along with those freedoms come our "free will" consequences.

It amazes me that when these consequences come, we often shift our thinking to "God is testing us." How ironic it is that we cry out the wrong plea before God, "Give me strength through this time of testing," or we explode social media with "Seeking prayer through time of testing," when we ought to be on our knees repenting and asking/begging/fasting for God's mercy. Furthermore, we should plead that He remember our humanity and see us in the light of his son Jesus.

David was a man considered by God "after his own heart." King David is one of my greatest Old Testament heroes. I often pray that I would be a "woman after God's own heart." However, David was human and clearly not above sin. If sin can have degrees, then David committed some of the greatest—adultery, deception, cover-up, murder, and misuse of power. And his sin cost him: the sword would never leave his home and the death of his son born to Bathsheba.

When David was confronted with his sin, he did not cry out how life was unfair and shift the understanding to "God is testing me." No, David went and pleaded with God to spare his son's life. He started a fast and lay on the ground for days, begging God to change his mind. Then when his son died, he got up, washed his face, put on clean clothes, and before he ate, he went and worshipped God. HE WENT AND WORSHIPPED GOD. Again, he did not complain that life is unfair, he did not point a finger, he was not misguided by claiming God was testing him, he did not shake his fist to the sky. He *accepted* and *worshipped*.

Here is the beauty in our free choices. When we repent and truly desire forgiveness, God is capable of taking our selfish, messed-up lives and still making something of them that glorifies Him. Even though our consequences will always be a healthy reminder, God is compassionate and loving. God gave King David and Bathsheba another son, Solomon. Furthermore, God will give you and me another as well, so let's get up, wash our faces, put on some clean clothes, and worship God!

> *Then David got up from the ground. After he had washed, put on lotions and changed his clothes, he went into the house of the Lord and Worshipped.*
>
> —2 Samuel 12:20

God's Hand

I am under vows to you, O God; I will present my thank offering to you. For you have delivered me from death and my feet from stumbling, that I may walk before God in the light of life.
—Psalm 56:12-13

WOW! What a ride these last few years have been! Yup! You better be prepared when you pray, "I want to know Christ as much as I can on this side of the cross." Or, "Lord Jesus, protect me ... *even* from myself." When you cry out to God and ask Him to circumcise your heart or pray to be a "woman after God's own heart," you better have your big-girl panties on because God will bring down all of Heaven to transport those prayers to life. Another prayer I have always prayed is, "God, help me to know ... that I know ... that I know with authority you exist so I can speak with passion for your Kingdom."

I am absolutely sure God has shaken His head at me many times. I am certain He has looked over at his Son Jesus and asked, "What are we going to do with her? What a stubborn one! I keep putting opportunities in front of her to rely on me, and she keeps running off doing it her way." So God decided to discipline me and have me take a three-year trip around the mountain of loneliness.

If you have more than one child, you will know that not all discipline works the same. I have three kids, and they required different corrections. One required, more often than not, the corporal punishment, for the other, isolation worked best, and with the third, I could just word him into obedience. I am a people person; the more the merrier. So God using the discipline of loneliness and stripping away those dependencies seems appropriate.

Going around this mountain has had some very rocky paths, some pitfalls, some murky areas, and some hard climbs. I am a very proactive person, so obedience to the subtle voice of God telling me to "be still," "stand down," and "lie passive" was extremely difficult to comprehend. I mean, does not God help those who help themselves? My hands-on approach to life, plowing forward and claiming the right to be "proactive," was not at all the words I was hearing in my spirit. So around the mountain I went!

God's hand on my life and His protection astonish me. The discipline has been painful, but my spiritual growth has been worth every lonely, dark, and despairing step. During this God-given time, I bowed to the Lordship of God and his sovereignty. I also came to realize I cannot walk by emotions but by what the Word of God says, truly a hard discipline to master. No matter what I want, desire, or feel, if it does not line up with God's Word, I must lay it down or never pick it up. I must stay true to what God has spoken to me and the biblical truth, even in opposition and disagreement from well-meaning (or not so well-meaning) people. When I bow to the Lordship of God, it is with the understanding that nothing on earth is more important than my relationship with God and his Son Jesus, which brings us to the story of the disciples in the boat.

The disciples were in a boat, and a great storm came up. Jesus was sleeping, so they went and woke him because they were afraid. However, before rebuking the winds, Jesus rebuked them for having little faith. I find this puzzling. The waves were crashing over the boat. Visually it looks as though they were about to go under. I am thinking being afraid is a normal reaction. I would also think going to Jesus is the right "faith-like" thing to do. But it is clear something is taking place that requires Jesus to call them out on their "lack of faith."

Thinking about this and asking Jesus for some insight, he gave me this understanding: there is a seed of faith in all believers, and we are to act and stand on this faith. The disciples had Jesus in the boat with them. What more did they need? I am thinking Jesus wanted them to just sit down and trust him. I can hear him say, "Why do you worry over the waves when I am here with you?" Sometimes in the midst of a really crazy storm, God gives the faith to do, move, "get busy." But there are times He tells us to sit down, wait, and pray.

I've always known why God took me around the mountain of loneliness, and I also knew what would have shortened the trip and what would have expedited the meadows and the sunshine on my face. "Stand down, be still, and don't move."

The waves of life can crash over us and maybe at times even take us under, but then let's hold our breath, hold to the seed of faith within, and look up through the water to fix our eyes on Jesus. When you come to a place that all earthly sensations pale in comparison to walking with Jesus and knowing his love, you will be able to hold your breath for a really, really long time. Believe me, I know. I've been doing it now for a while.

> *In your struggle against sin, you have not yet resisted to the point of shedding your blood. And you have forgotten that word of encouragement that addresses you as son:*
>
> *"My son, do not make light of the Lord's disciplines, and do not lose heart when he rebukes you, because the Lord disciplines those he loves, and he punishes everyone he accepts as a son.*
>
> *—Hebrews 12:4-6*

Where Are You Now

It is better to go to the house of mourning than to go to a house of feasting, for death is the destiny of every man; the living should take this to heart.

—Ecclesiastes 7:2

A body lying lifeless demands a reality check to every person viewing this once full-of-life spirited person. Although we see the body before us, we know the person is gone and we mourn. Death is a sobering reality, an inescapable truth, and I would dare say scary to most when facing it for themselves.

This may seem a little morbid or strange, but I enjoy walking through cemeteries. I find it to be introspective and a great sense of wonder as I think of the once lived lives. As I stop and read headstones; the date of birth and the date of death, I can't help but think, "what took place between these dates?" I will sometimes squat down and brush the grass with my hand and think of the person below me: *Who were you? Did you love? Were you loved? Did you grow up happy? Poor? Wealthy? What were your dreams? Did you reach them? How about your sorrows or discouragements; did you handle them with courage or did they defeat you? Were you a good person, bad, hateful, evil, or a loving person? Where are you now?*

If you were told you had a year to live, or a few months, or just a couple of weeks, what would you do? Our first instinct is to say, I'd live life to the fullest. We'd grab our loved ones and hold them tight. We'd find our list of things we have always wanted to do and begin doing them. I am reminded of a movie I watched that absolutely made me sob. I completely bawled my eyes out, *Phoenix and Griffin*. A man and woman met in a college psychology class on death. They told each other they were taking the class for their degree when in actuality they were both diagnosed with a terminal illness and had only months to live. With this unknown reality between them, they did romantic crazy things. They set out to accomplish their bucket list and somewhere in the midst, they fell in love. (Spoiler alert, they both ended up dying, and I cried myself to sleep!)

Over the years, I have seen death up close and from a distance. It always leaves me with a dismal knowledge on how fast time flies, how short our lives are, and thoughts of eternity. I am left with asking myself the same question I just asked you, "If I had only a year or less to live, what would I do?" Initially, my response was like most: grab my bucket list and go! However, when I really thought about it, I realized I have all eternity to see God's incredible mountains and oceans. I have all eternity to richly enjoy God's created beauty. I have all eternity to enjoy the pleasures God intended man to have. However, I don't have all eternity to tell people about Jesus. So instead I'd grab every soul I could on my way out (up); starting with my kids, grandkids, friends, and all the people in-between. I'd shout from the street corners, "Jesus saves" (I know a little over the top).

When we are told life is short, it changes our focus. Let me say, I don't think there is any right or wrong answer to this question except "that is what we should be doing now." It does not matter what you would do, but it matters why you would do what you do. It is always about the motive of the heart. We should be living a vertical focus while living a horizontal life.

Another strangely odd question asked to several of us sitting around one day was: "What would you want written on your headstone?" There were several quick answers. However, as I sat there listening, I felt the desire to ask God about what He would want me to put on my headstone. So I did, and these sweet words were whispered to me:

Sonia Lee Beckwith
Born June 12, 1959, my body died _____
But because Jesus Christ died and rose again, I live!
John 3:16

I envision someone, like myself, walking through a cemetery and stumbling upon my grave site reading these words. They may be puzzled if they have no understanding of eternity or who Jesus is. However, if they know the redemptive truth, I can envision a little corner grin breaking into a huge smile while looking to the sky.

What if he stumbles upon your grave site? What if he takes a moment to kneel down to contemplate your life lived between the dates he just read? What would the answers be to his many questions? Did you know Jesus, the spotless sacrifice? Did you believe in the cross? Was Jesus your Lord and Savior? *"Where are you now?"*

> *But because of his great love for us, God who is rich in mercy, made us alive with Christ even when we were dead in transgression; it is by grace you have been saved. And God raised us up with Christ and seated us with him in the heavenly realms in Christ Jesus, in order that in the coming ages he might show the incomparable riches of this grace, expressed in his kindness to us in Christ Jesus.*
>
> —*Ephesians 2:4-7*

God Gave Me Stories

So there you have it. All the preceding is from a moment in time when I was sitting in a chapel service, once again spellbound by the speaker, the Holy Spirit gripping my heart by every word spoken and pointing my attention to Christ.

I remember Jesus speaking to me and my thinking how amazing this person was and the incredible stories being shared that day. As the Holy Spirit spoke to my heart, I felt God was singling me out. I remember saying, "But I don't have any stories. What would I possibly have to say for you, Lord?"

I am now fifty-five years old. It is Christmas Day 2014. In the last six months, I have never been on my knees more. I have never cried more (grief, I am starting to cry now) over God's incredible desire for man to see his son Jesus. I believe I am an evangelist at heart, for all I seem to care about is the salvation of man; second to that is man's spiritual growth.

I don't have any clue what these stories will mean to you. I pray, though, as the Holy Spirit moved me many years ago, he will move you today. I pray you will desire to strive and live a life pleasing to God. I pray you will open your Bible to read, search, and study. I pray you will find time daily to talk with Jesus and God. That you find time to worship and actively seek ways to serve God, be it a smile, a sincere hello, offering a "glass of water," or standing behind the pulpit teaching the Word.

My final thoughts: If you are part of my life and have known me for any length of time, you will certainly know I am not without sin. I make no claim to "not having skeletons in the closet." However,

I do make the claim that I am fully forgiven by God through his son Jesus. Based on this, my life is open. I know I have selfishly and blatantly sinned, but here is the thing (just in case you are trying to justify your sin based on mine): my sin does not make your sin right. When we sin, grace is given. BUT WE DON'T SIN BECAUSE GRACE IS GIVEN.

Thank you, God, that many years ago you heard the prayer of a young girl's heart, "But I don't have any stories."

So GOD GAVE ME STORIES.

In thinking through my stories, I began hearing this theme:

We Must Remember God's

Voice
His commandments
His glory
His knowledge
His ministering angels
His discipline
His strength
His wisdom
His sovereignty
His healing power
His touch
His holiness
His love
His faithfulness
His coming judgment
His Son

Eternity

About the Author

I was born and raised in Michigan; however, I have had the privilege to live in Frisco, Texas, for the past thirty years. I have three wonderful adult children who have given me eleven amazing grandkids. I work as an independent hairstylist, and from this platform, I have had the opportunity to share Christ over the past twenty years.

I came to a saving grace of God through my Lord, Jesus Christ, when I was seventeen. Since that time, I have always been eternal-focused. I have always viewed this life on earth so very short in comparison to how enormous and unimaginable the span of eternity is. We are all just a speck, a very small drop of water in the ocean. Life must have purpose beyond our earthly existence. I have found this meaningful peace in Jesus. As a Christian, God is trustworthy as we "lie passive in His hands," in His will, in His purpose as we walk this earth.

CPSIA information can be obtained
at www.ICGtesting.com
Printed in the USA
LVOW11s0448030817
543668LV00001B/45/P